FROM THE ARCHIVES OF THE

MUSLIM BROTHERHOOD
IN AMERICA

AN EXPLANATORY MEMORANDUM
ON THE GENERAL STRATEGIC GOAL
FOR THE GROUP IN NORTH AMERICA

For more information about this book visit
SECUREFREEDOM.ORG

*An Explanatory Memorandum: From the Archives of the Muslim Brotherhood
in America* is published in the United States by the Center for
Security Policy Press, a division of the Center for Security Policy.

ISBN 978-0-9822947-1-0

THE CENTER FOR SECURITY POLICY
1901 Pennsylvania Avenue, Suite 201
Washington, DC 20006
Phone: (202) 835-9077
Email: info@securefreedom.org
For more information, please see securefreedom.org

Book design by David Reaboi.

CONTENTS

"The process of settlement is a 'Civilization-Jihadist Process' with all the word means. The Ikhwan [Muslim Brotherhood] must understand that their work in America is a kind of grand jihad in eliminating and destroying the Western civilization from within and "sabotaging" its miserable house by their hands and the hands of the believers so that it is eliminated and God's religion is made victorious over all other religions."

From the **Explanatory Memorandum**

In August of 2004, an alert Maryland Transportation Authority Police officer observed a woman wearing traditional Islamic garb videotaping the support structures of the Chesapeake Bay Bridge, and conducted a traffic stop. The driver of the vehicle was identified as Ismail Elbarasse and detained on an outstanding material witness warrant issued in Chicago, Illinois, in connection with fundraising for Hamas.

The FBI's Washington Field Office subsequently executed a search warrant on Elbarasse's residence in Annandale, Virginia. In the basement of his home, a hidden sub-basement was found. The contents of the sub-basement proved to be the archives of the Muslim Brotherhood in North America.

Among the 80 banker-boxes worth of documents discovered there were papers that confirmed what investigators and counterterrorism experts had long suspected and contended about the myriad Muslim-American groups in the United States: nearly all of them are controlled by the Muslim Brotherhood.

Therefore, in accordance with the supremacist Islamic doctrine known as shariah, such groups are hostile to this country, its Constitution and freedoms. The documents make clear the groups' sole objectives are to implement Islamic law in America in furtherance of re-establishing the global caliphate.

One of the most important of these documents made public to date was entered into evidence during the Holy Land Foundation trial. It amounted to the Muslim Brotherhood's strategic plan for the United States and was entitled, "An Explanatory Memorandum: On the General Strategic Goal for the Group in North America."

The Explanatory Memorandum was written in 1991 by a member of the Board of Directors for the Muslim Brotherhood in North America and senior Hamas leader named Mohamed Akram. It had been approved by the Brotherhood's Shura Council and Organizational Conference and was meant for internal review by the Brothers' leadership in Egypt. It was certainly not intended for public consumption, particularly in the targeted society: the United States.

For these reasons, the memo constitutes a kind of Rosetta stone for the Muslim Brotherhood, its goals, modus operandi and infrastructure in America. It is arguably the single most important vehicle for understanding a secretive organization and should, therefore, be considered required reading for policy-makers and the public, alike.

To that end, the Center for Security Policy published this document in its entirety as an appendix in the highly acclaimed 2010 Report of Team B II entitled, *Shariah: The Threat to America (An Exercise in Competitive Analysis)*. The book provides a wealth of explanatory information and is recommended as a resource concerning the ideology or doctrine that inspires the Muslim Brotherhood and other Islamists—shariah—and the ways in which the Brothers have been advancing its supremacist agenda, here and abroad.

In the hope of encouraging the widest possible readership of the Explanatory Memorandum, the Center has reproduced it here in a freestanding form. Passages that are particularly noteworthy are highlighted.

Among those warranting special attention are what amounts to the mission statement of the Muslim Brotherhood in America:

> The process of settlement is a "Civilization-Jihadist Process" with all the word means. The Ikhwan [Arabic for Muslim Brotherhood] must understand that their work in America is a kind of grand jihad in eliminating and destroying the Western civilization from within and "sabotaging" its miserable house by their hands and the hands of the believers so that it is eliminated and God's religion is made victorious over all other religions.

As Team B II observed:

> In other words, the Ikhwan's strategy for destroying the United States is to get us, specifically our leadership, to do the Muslim Brotherhood's bidding. The

Ikhwan intends to conduct civilization jihad by coopting our leadership into believing a counterfactual understanding of Islam and the nature of the Muslim Brotherhood, thereby manipulating or coercing these leaders to enforce the MB narrative on their subordinates.

Another extraordinarily important element of the Memorandum is its attachment. Under the heading "A List of Our Organizations and Organizations of Our Friends," Akram helpfully identified 29 groups as Muslim Brotherhood fronts. Many of them are even now, some twenty-two years later, still among the most prominent Muslim-American organizations in the United States.

Worryingly, the senior representatives of these groups are routinely identified by U.S. officials as "leaders" of the Muslim community in this country, to be treated as "partners" in "countering violent extremism" and other outreach initiatives. Obviously, this list suggests such treatment translates into vehicles for deep penetration of the American government and civil society.

We urge the readers of this pamphlet to share it with others—family members, friends, business associates and most especially those in a position to help adopt policies that will secure our country against the threat posed by shariah and its most effective and aggressive promoters, the Muslim Brotherhood.

Frank J. Gaffney, Jr.
February 2013
Washington, DC

The following Muslim Brotherhood document was entered into evidence in the U.S. v Holy Land Foundation trial, and is a primary source threat document that provides new insights into global jihad organizations like the Muslim Brotherhood. These documents (covered extensively in chapter four) define the structure and outline of domestic jihad threat entities, associated non-governmental organizations and potential terrorist or insurgent support systems. The Memorandum also describes aspects of the global jihad's strategic information warfare campaign and indications of its structure, reach and activities. It met evidentiary standards to be admissible as evidence in a Federal Court of law.

In the original document, the first 16 pages are in the original Arabic and the second are English translations of the same. It is dated May 22, 1991 and titled "An Explanatory Memorandum on the General Strategic Goal for the Group in North America" (Memorandum). The document includes an Attachment 1 that contains "a list of our organizations and the organizations of our friends."

The Memorandum expressly recognizes the Muslim Brotherhood (*Ikhwan*) as the controlling element of these organizations and expressly identifies the Muslim Brotherhood as the leadership element in implementing the strategic goals. The Memorandum is reproduced here in its official Federal Court translation, as Government Exhibit 003-0085 3:04-CR-240-G in U.S. v Holy Land Foundation, et al. with punctuation, line spacing and spelling intact.

بسم الله الرحمن الرحيم

الحمد لله رب العالمين و الصلاة و السلام على سيد المرسلين

مذكرة تفسيرية

للهدف الإستراتيجيّ العام للجماعة في أمريكا الشمالية

١٩٩١/٥/٢٢

المحتويات :

AN EXPLANATORY MEMORANDUM ON THE GENERAL STRATEGIC GOAL FOR THE GROUP IN NORTH AMERICA:

5/22/1991

In the name of God, the Beneficent, the Merciful
Thanks be to God, Lord of the Two Worlds
And Blessed are the Pious
The beloved brother/The General Masul, may God keep him
The beloved brother/secretary of the Shura Council, may God keep him
The beloved brothers/Mernbers of the Shura Council, may God keep them
God's peace, mercy and blessings be upon you. ... . To proceed,

I ask Almighty God that you, your families and those whom you love around you are in the best of conditions, pleasing to God, glorified His name be.

I send this letter of mine to you hoping that it would seize your attention and receive your good care as you are the people of responsibility and those to whom trust is given. Between your hands is an "Explanatory Memorandum" which I put effort in writing down so that it is not locked in the chest and the mind, and so that I can share with you a portion of the responsibility in leading the Group in this country.

What might have encouraged me to submit the memorandum in this time in particular is my feeling of a "glimpse of hope" and the beginning of good tidings which bring the good news that we have embarked on a new stage of Islamic activism stages in this continent.

The papers which are between your hands are not abundant extravagance, imaginations or hallucinations which passed in the mind of one of your brothers, but they are rather hopes, ambitions and challenges that I hope that you share some or most of which with me. I do not claim their infallibility or absolute correctness, but they are an attempt which requires study, outlook, detailing and rooting from you.

My request to my brothers is to read the memorandum and to write what they wanted of comments and corrections, keeping in mind that what is between your hands is not strange or a new submission without a root, but rather an attempt to interpret and explain some of what came in the long-term plan which we approved and adopted in our council and our conference in the year (1987).

So, my honorable brother, do not rush to throw these papers away due to your many occupations and worries, All what I'm asking of you is to read them and to comment on them hoping that we might continue together the project of our plan and our Islamic work in this part of the world. Should you do that, I would be thankful and grateful to you.

I also ask my honorable brother, the Secretary of the Council, to add the subject of the memorandum on the Council agenda in its coming meeting.

May God reward you good and keep you for His Daw'a

Your brother Mohamed Akram

In the name of God, the Beneficent, the Merciful
Thanks be to God, Lord of the Two Worlds
And Blessed are the Pious

Subject: A project for an explanatory memorandum for the General Strategic goal for the Group in North America mentioned in the long-term plan

One: The Memorandum is derived from:

1. The general strategic goal of the Group in America which was approved by the Shura Council and the Organizational Conference for the year [1987] is "Enablement of Islam in North America, meaning: establishing an effective and a stable Islamic Movement led by the

Muslim Brotherhood which adopts Muslims' causes domestically and globally, and which works to expand the observant Muslim base, aims at unifying and directing Muslims' efforts, presents Islam as a civilization alternative, and supports the global Islamic State wherever it is".

2. The priority that is approved by the Shura Council for the work of the Group in its current and former session which is "Settlement".

3. The positive development with the brothers in the Islamic Circle in an attempt to reach a unity of merger.

4. The constant need for thinking and future planning, an attempt to read it and working to "shape" the present to comply and suit the needs and challenges of the future.

5. The paper of his eminence, the General Masul, may God keep him, which he recently sent to the members of the Council.

Two: An Introduction to the Explanatory Memorandum:

In order to begin with the explanation, we must "summon" the following question and place it in front of our eyes as its relationship is important and necessary with the strategic goal and the explanation project we are embarking on. The question we are facing is: "How do you like to see the Islam Movement in North America in ten years?", or "taking along" the following sentence when planning and working, "Islamic Work in North America in the year (2000): A Strategic Vision".

Also, we must summon and take along "elements" of the general strategic goal of the Group in North America and I will intentionally repeat them in numbers. They are:

[1 - Establishing an effective and stable Islamic Movement led by the Muslim Brotherhood.

2 - Adopting Muslims' causes domestically and globally.

3 - Expanding the observant Muslim base.

4- Unifying and directing Muslims' efforts.

5 - Presenting Islam as a civilization alternative

6 - Supporting the establishment of the global Islamic State wherever it is].

- It must be stressed that it has become clear and emphatically known that all is in agreement that we must "settle" or "enable" Islam and its Movement in this part of the world.

- Therefore, a joint understanding of the meaning of settlement or enablement must be adopted, through which and on whose basis we explain the general strategic goal with its six elements for the Group in North America.

Three: The Concept of Settlement:

This term was mentioned in the Group's "dictionary" and documents with various meanings in spite of the fact that everyone meant one thing with it. We believe that the understanding of the essence is the same and we will attempt here to give the word and its "meanings" a practical explanation with a practical Movement tone, and not a philosophical linguistic explanation, while stressing that this explanation of ours is not complete until our explanation of "the process" of settlement itself is understood which is mentioned in the following paragraph. We briefly say the following:

Settlement:	"That Islam and its Movement become a part of the homeland it lives in".
Establishment:	"That Islam turns into firmly-rooted organizations on whose bases civilization, structure and testimony are built".
Stability:	"That Islam is stable in the land on which its people move".
Enablement:	"That Islam is enabled within the souls, minds and the lives of the people of the country in which it moves".

| Rooting: | "That Islam is resident and not a passing thing, or rooted "entrenched" in the soil of the spot where it moves and not a strange plant to it". |

Four: The Process of Settlement:

- In order for Islam and its Movement to become "a part of the homeland" in which it lives, "stable" in its land, "rooted" in the spirits and minds of its people, "enabled" in the live of its society and has firmly-established "organizations" on which the Islamic structure is built and with which the testimony of civilization is achieved, the Movement must plan and struggle to obtain "the keys" and the tools of this process in carry out this grand mission as a "Civilization Jihadist" responsibility which lies on the shoulders of Muslims and - on top of them - the Muslim Brotherhood in this country. Among these keys and tools are the following:

1- Adopting the concept of settlement and understanding its practical meanings:

The Explanatory Memorandum focused on the Movement and the realistic dimension of the process of settlement and its practical meanings without paying attention to the difference in understanding between the resident and the non-resident, or who is the settled and the non-settled and we believe that what was mentioned in the long-term plan in that regards suffices.

2 - Making a fundamental shift in our thinking and mentality in order to suit the challenges of the settlement mission.

What is meant with the shift - which is a positive expression - is responding to the grand challenges of the settlement issues. We believe that any transforming response begins with the method of thinking and its center, the brain, first. In order to clarify what is meant with the shift as a key to qualify us to enter the field of settlement, we say very briefly that the following must be accomplished:

- A shift from the "amputated" partial thinking mentality to the "continuous" comprehensive mentality.

- A shift from the mentality of caution and reservation to the mentality of risk and controlled liberation.

- A shift from the mentality of the elite Movement to the mentality of the popular Movement.

- A shift from the mentality of preaching and guidance to the mentality of building and testimony

- A shift from the single opinion mentality to the multiple opinion mentality.

- A shift from the collision mentality to the absorption mentality.

- A shift from the individual mentality to the team mentality.

- A shift from the anticipation mentality to the initiative mentality.

- A shift from the hesitation mentality to the decisiveness mentality.

- A shift from the principles mentality to the programs mentality.

- A shift from the abstract ideas mentality the true organizations mentality

[This is the core point and the essence of the memorandum].

3- Understanding the historical stages in which the Islamic Ikhwani activism went through in this country:

The writer of the memorandum believes that understanding and comprehending the historical stages of the Islamic activism which was led and being led by the Muslim Brotherhood in this continent is a very important key in working towards settlement, through which the Group observes its march, the direction of its movement and the curves and turns of its road. We will suffice here with mentioning the title for each of these stages [The title expresses the prevalent characteristic of the stage] [Details maybe mentioned in another future study]. Most likely, the stages are:

A - The stage of searching for self and determining the identity.

B - The stage of inner build-up and tightening the organization.

C - The stage of mosques and the Islamic centers.

D - The stage of building the Islamic organizations - the first phase.

E - The stage of building the Islamic schools - the first phase.

F - The stage of thinking about the overt Islamic Movement - the first phase.

G - The stage of openness to the other Islamic movements and attempting to reach a formula for dealing with them - the first phase.

H - The stage of reviving and establishing the Islamic organizations - the second phase.

We believe that the Group is embarking on this stage in its second phase as it has to open the door and enter as it did the first time.

4- Understanding the role of the Muslim Brother in North America:

The process of settlement is a "Civilization-Jihadist Process" with all the word means. The Ikhwan must understand that their work in America is a kind of grand Jihad in eliminating and destroying the

Western civilization from within and "sabotaging" its miserable house by their hands and the hands of the believers so that it is eliminated and God's religion is made victorious over all other religions. Without this level of understanding, we are not up to this challenge and have not prepared ourselves for Jihad yet. It is a Muslim's destiny to perform Jihad and work wherever he is and wherever he lands until the final hour comes, and there is no escape from that destiny except for those who chose to slack. But, would the slackers and the Mujahedeen be equal.

5- Understanding that we cannot perform the settlement mission by ourselves or away from people:

A mission as significant and as huge as the settlement mission needs magnificent and exhausting efforts. With their capabilities, human, financial and scientific resources, the Ikhwan will not be able to carry out this mission alone or away from people and he who believes that is wrong, and God knows best. As for the role of the Ikhwan, it is the initiative, pioneering, leadership, raising the banner and pushing people in that direction. They are then to work to employ, direct and unify Muslims' efforts and powers for this process. In order to do that, we must possess a mastery of the art of "coalitions", the art of "absorption" and the principles of "cooperation".

6- The necessity of achieving a union and balanced gradual merger between private work and public work:

We believe that what was written about this subject is many and is enough. But, it needs a time and a practical frame so that what is needed is achieved in a gradual and a balanced way that is compatible with the process of settlement.

7- The conviction that the success of the settlement of Islam and its Movement in this country is a success to the global Islamic Movement and a true support for the sought-after state, God willing:

There is a conviction - with which this memorandum disagrees - that our focus in attempting to settle Islam in this country will lead to negligence in our duty towards the global Islamic Movement in supporting its project to establish the state. We believe that the reply is in two segments: One - The success of the Movement in America in establishing an observant Islamic base with power and effectiveness will be the best support and aid to the global Movement project.

And the second - is the global Movement has not succeeded yet in "distributing roles" to its branches, stating what is the needed from them as one of the participants or contributors to the project to establish the global Islamic state. The day this happens, the children of the American Ikhwani branch will have far-reaching impact and positions that make the ancestors proud.

8- Absorbing Muslims and winning them with all of their factions and colors in America and Canada for the settlement project, and making it their cause, future and the basis of their Islamic life in this part of the world:

This issues requires from us to learn "the art of dealing with the others", as people are different and people in many colors. We need to adopt the principle which says, "Take from people ... the best they have", their best specializations, experiences, arts, energies and abilities. By people here we mean those within or without the ranks of individuals and organizations. The policy of "taking" should be with what achieves the strategic goal and the settlement process. But the big challenge in front of us is: how to connect them all in "the orbit" of our plan and "the circle" of our Movement in order to achieve "the core" of our interest. To me, there is no choice for us other than alliance and mutual understanding of those who desire from our religion and those who agree from our belief in work. And the U.S. Islamic arena is full of those waiting..., the pioneers.

What matters is bringing people to the level of comprehension of the challenge that is facing us as Muslims in this country, conviction of our settlement project, and understanding the benefit of agreement, cooperation and alliance. At that time, if we ask for money, a lot of it would come, and if we ask for men, they would come in lines, What matters is that our plan is "the criterion and the balance" in our relationship with others.

Here, two points must be noted; the first one: we need to comprehend and understand the balance of the Islamic powers in the U.S. arena [and this might be the subject of a future study]. The second point: what we reached with the brothers in "ICNA" is considered a step in the right direction, the beginning of good and the first drop that requires growing and guidance.

9- Re-examining our organizational and administrative bodies, the type of leadership and the method of selecting it with what suits the challenges of the settlement mission:

The memorandum will be silent about details regarding this item even though it is logical and there is a lot to be said about it.

10- Growing and developing our resources and capabilities, our financial and human resources with what suits the magnitude of the grand mission:

If we examined the human and the financial resources the Ikhwan alone own in this country, we and others would feel proud and glorious. And if we add to them the resources of our friends and allies, those who circle in our orbit and those waiting on our banner, we would realize that we are able to open the door to settlement and walk through it seeking to make Almighty God's word the highest.

11- Utilizing the scientific method in planning, thinking and preparation of studies needed for the process of settlement:

Yes, we need this method, and we need many studies which aid in this civilization Jihadist operation. We will mention some of them briefly:

- The history of the Islamic presence in America.

- The history of the Islamic Ikhwani presence in America.

- Islamic movements, organizations and organizations: analysis and criticism.

- The phenomenon of the Islamic centers and schools: challenges, needs and statistics.

- Islamic minorities.

- Muslim and Arab communities.

- The U.S. society: make-up and politics.

- The U.S. society's view of Islam and Muslims ... And many other studies which we can direct our brothers and allies to prepare, either through their academic studies or through their educational centers or organizational tasking. What is important is that we start.

12- **Agreeing on a flexible, balanced and a clear "mechanism" to implement the process of settlement within a specific, gradual and balanced "time frame" that is in-line with the demands and challenges of the process of settlement.**

13- **Understanding the U.S. society from its different aspects an understanding that "qualifies" us to perform the mission of settling our Dawa' in its country "and growing it" on its land.**

14- **Adopting a written "jurisprudence" that includes legal and movement bases, principles, policies and interpretations which are suitable for the needs and challenges of the process of settlement.**

15- **Agreeing on "criteria" and balances to be a sort of "antennas" or "the watch tower" in order to make sure that all of our priorities, plans, programs, bodies, leadership, monies and activities march towards the process of the settlement.**

16- Adopting a practical, flexible formula through which our central work complements our domestic work.

[Items 12 through 16 will be detailed later].

17- Understanding the role and the nature of work of "The Islamic Center" in every city with what achieves the goal of the process of settlement:

The center we seek is the one which constitutes the "axis" of our Movement, the "perimeter" of the circle of our work, our "balance center", the "base" for our rise and our "Dar al-Arqam" to educate us, prepare us and supply our battalions in addition to being the "niche" of our prayers.

This is in order for the Islamic center to turn - in action not in words - into a seed "for a small Islamic society" which is a reflection and a mirror to our central organizations. The center ought to turn into a "beehive" which produces sweet honey. Thus, the Islamic center would turn into a place for study, family, battalion, course, seminar, visit, sport, school, social club, women gathering, kindergarten for male and female youngsters, the office of the domestic political resolution, and the center for distributing our newspapers, magazines, books and our audio and visual tapes.

In brief we say: we would like for the Islamic center to become "The House of Dawa'" and "the general center" in deeds first before name. As much as we own and direct these centers at the continent level, we can say we are marching successfully towards the settlement of Dawa' in this country.

Meaning that the "center's" role should be the same as the "mosque's" role during the time of God's prophet, God's prayers and peace be upon him, when he marched to "settle" the Dawa' in its first generation in Madina. from the mosque, he drew the Islamic life and provided to the world the most magnificent and fabulous civilization humanity knew.

This mandates that, eventually, the region, the branch and the Usra turn into "operations rooms" for planning, direction, monitoring and leadership for the Islamic center in order to be a role model to be followed.

18- Adopting a system that is based on "selecting" workers, "role distribution" and "assigning" positions and responsibilities is based on specialization, desire and need with what achieves the process of settlement and contributes to its success.

19- Turning the principle of dedication for the Masuls of main positions within the Group into a rule, a basis and a policy in work. Without it, the process of settlement might be stalled [Talking about this point requires more details and discussion].

20- Understanding the importance of the "Organizational" shift in our Movement work, and doing Jihad in order to achieve it in the real world with what serves the process of settlement and expedites its results, God Almighty's willing:

The reason this paragraph was delayed is to stress its utmost importance as it constitutes the heart and the core of this memorandum. It also constitutes the practical aspect and the true measure of our success or failure in our march towards settlement. The talk about the organizations and the "organizational" mentality or phenomenon does not require much details. It suffices to say that the first pioneer of this phenomenon was our prophet Mohamed, God's peace, mercy and blessings be upon him, as he placed the foundation for the first civilized organization which is the mosque, which truly became "the comprehensive organization". And this was done by the pioneer of the contemporary Islamic Dawa', Imam martyr Hasan al-Banna, may God have mercy on him, when he and his brothers felt the need to "re-establish" Islam and its movement anew, leading him to establish organizations with all their kinds: economic, social, media, scouting, professional and even the military ones. We must say that we are in a country which understands no language other than the language of the organizations, and one which does not respect or give weight to any group without effective, functional and strong organizations.

It is good fortune that there are brothers among us who have this "trend", mentality or inclination to build the organizations who have beat us by action and words which leads us to dare say honestly what Sadat in Egypt once said, "We want to build a country of organizations" - a word of right he meant wrong with. I say to my brothers, let us raise the banner of truth to establish right "We want to establish the Group of organizations", as without it we will not able to put our feet on the true path.

- And in order for the process of settlement to be completed, we must plan and work from now to equip and prepare ourselves, our brothers, our apparatuses, our sections and our committees in order to turn into comprehensive organizations in a gradual and balanced way that is suitable with the need and the reality. What encourages us to do that - in addition to the aforementioned - is that we possess "seeds" for each organization from the organization we call for [See attachment number (1)].

- All we need is to tweak them, coordinate their work, collect their elements and merge their efforts with others and then connect them with the comprehensive plan we seek. For instance, We have a seed for a "comprehensive media and art" organization: we own a print + advanced typesetting machine + audio and visual center + art production office + magazines in Arabic and English [The Horizons, The Hope, The Politicians, Ila Falastine, Press Clips, al-Zaytouna, Palestine Monitor, Social Sciences Magazines...] + art band + photographers + producers + programs anchors +journalists + in addition to other media and art experiences".

Another example:

We have a seed for a "comprehensive Dawa' educational" organization: We have the Daw'a section in ISNA + Dr. Jamal Badawi Foundation + the center run by brother Harned al-Ghazali + the Dawa' center the Dawa' Committee and brother Shaker al-Sayyed are seeking to establish now + in addition to other Daw'a efforts here and there...".

And this applies to all the organizations we call on establishing.

- The big challenge that is ahead of us is how to turn these seeds or "scattered" elements into comprehensive, stable, "settled" organizations that are connected with our Movement and which fly in our orbit and take orders from ow guidance. This does not prevent - but calls for - each central organization to have its local branches but its connection with the Islamic center in the city is a must.

- What is needed is to seek to prepare the atmosphere and the means to achieve "the merger" so that the sections, the committees, the regions, the branches and the Usras are eventually the heart and the core of these organizations.

Or, for the shift and the change to occur as follows:

1 - The Movement Department + The Secretariat Department — The Organizational & Administrative Organization - The General Center

2- Education Department + Dawa'a Com. — Dawa' and Educational Organization

3- Sisters Department — The Women's Organization

4- The Financial Department + Investment Committee + The Endowment — The Economic Organization

5- Youth Department + Youths Organizations Department — Youth Organizations

6- The Social Committee + Matrimony Committee + Mercy Foundation — The Social Organization

7- The Security Committee — The Security Organization

8- The Political Depart. + Palestine Com. — The Political Organization

9- The Group's Court + The Legal Com. — The Judicial Organization

10- Domestic Work Department — Its work is to be distributed to the rest of the organizations

11 - Our magazines + the print + our art band — The Media and Art Organization

12- The Studies Association + The Publication House + Dar al-Kitab — The Intellectual & Cultural Organization

13- Scientific and Medial societies — Scientific, Educational & Professional Organization

14- The Organizational Conference — The Islamic-American Founding Conference

15- The Shura Council + Planning Com. — The Shura Council for the Islamic-American Movement

16- The Executive Office — The Executive Office of the Islamic-American Movement

17- The General Masul — Chairman of the Islamic Movement and its official Spokesman

18- The regions, branches & Usras — Field leaders of organizations & Islamic centers

Five: Comprehensive Settlement Organization:

- We would then seek and struggle in order to make each one of these above-mentioned organizations a "comprehensive organization" throughout the days and the years, and as long as we are destined to be in this country. What is important is that we put the foundation and we will be followed by peoples and generations that would finish the march and the road but with a clearly-defined guidance.

And, in order for us to clarify what we mean with the comprehensive, specialized organization, we mention here the characteristics and traits of each organization of the "promising" organizations.

1- From the Dawa' and educational aspect [The Dawa' and Educational Organization]: to include:

- The Organization to spread the Dawa' (Central and local branches).

- An institute to graduate Callers and Educators.

- Scholars, Callers, Educators, Preachers and Program Anchors,

- Art and communication technology, Conveyance and Dawa'.

- A television station.

- A specialized Dawa' magazine.

- A radio station.

- The Higher Islamic Council for Callers and Educators.

- The Higher Council for Mosques and Islamic Centers.

- Friendship Societies with the other religions... and things like that.

2- Politically [The Political Organization]: to include:

- A central political party.

- Local political offices.

- Political symbols.

- Relationships and alliances.

- The American Organization for Islamic Political Action

- Advanced Information Centers....and things like that.

3- Media [The Media and Art Organization]: to include:

- A daily newspaper.

- Weekly, monthly and seasonal magazines.

- Radio stations.

- Television programs.

- Audio and visual centers.

- A magazine for the Muslim child.

- A magazine for the Muslim woman.

- A print and typesetting machines.

- A production office.

- A photography and recording studio

- Art bands for acting, chanting and theater.

- A marketing and art production office... and things like that.

4- Economically [The Economic Organization]: to include:

- An Islamic Central bank.

- Islamic endowments.

- Investment projects.

- An organization for interest-free loans... and things like that.

5- Scientifically and Professionally [The Scientific, Educational and Professional Organization]: to include:

- Scientific research centers.

- Technical organizations and vocational training.

- An Islamic university.

- Islamic schools.

- A council for education and scientific research.

- Centers to train teachers.

- Scientific societies in schools.

- An office for academic guidance.

- A body for authorship and Islamic curricula....and things like that.

6- Culturally and Intellectually [The Cultural and Intellectual Organization]: to include:

- A center for studies and research.

- Cultural and intellectual foundations such as [The Social Scientists Society - Scientists and Engineers Society....]

- An organization for Islamic thought and culture.

- A publication, translation and distribution house for Islamic books.

- An office for archiving, history and authentication

- The project to translate the Noble Quran, the Noble Sayings... and things like that.

7- Socially [The Social-Charitable Organization]: to include:

- Social clubs for the youths and the community's sons and daughters

- Local societies for social welfare and the services are tied to the Islamic centers

- The Islamic Organization to Combat the Social Ills of the U.S. Society

- Islamic houses project

- Matrimony and family cases office... and things like that.

8- Youths [The Youth Organization]: to include:

- Central and local youths foundations.

- Sports teams and clubs

- Scouting teams... and things like that.

9- Women [The Women Organization]: to include:

- Central and local women societies.

- Organizations of training, vocational and housekeeping.

- An organization to train female preachers.

- Islamic kindergartens... and things like that.

10- Organizationally and Administratively [The Administrative and Organizational Organization]: to include:

- An institute for training, growth, development and planning

- Prominent experts in this field

- Work systems, bylaws and charters fit for running the most complicated bodies and organizations

- A periodic magazine in Islamic development and administration.

- Owning camps and halls for the various activities.

- A data, polling and census bank.

- An advanced communication network.

- An advanced archive for our heritage and production... and things like that.

11- Security [The Security Organization]: to include:

- Clubs for training and learning self-defense techniques.

- A center which is concerned with the security issues [Technical, intellectual, technological and human]....and things like that.

12- Legally [The Legal Organization]: to include:

- A Central Jurisprudence Council.

- A Central Islamic Court.

- Muslim Attorneys Society.

- The Islamic Foundation for Defense of Muslims' Rights... and things like that.

And success is by God.

Attachment number (1)
A list of our organizations and the organizations of our friends
[Imagine if t they all march according to one plan!!!]

1- ISNA	ISLAMIC SOCIETY OF NORTH AMERICA
2- MSA	MUSLIM STUDENTS' ASSOCIATION
3- MCA	THE MUSLIM COMMUNITIES ASSOCIATION
4- AMSS	THE ASSOCIATION OF MUSLIM SOCIAL SCIENTISTS
5- AMSE	THE ASSOCIATION OF MUSLIM SCIENTISTS AND ENGINEERS
6- IMA	ISLAMIC MEDICAL ASSOCIATION
7- ITC	ISLAMIC TEACHING CENTER
8- NAIT	NORTH AMERICAN ISLAMIC TRUST
9- FID	FOUNDATION FOR INTERNATIONAL DEVELOPMENT
10- IHC	ISLAMIC HOUSING COOPERATIVE
11- ICD	ISLAMIC CENTERS DIVISION
12- ATP	AMERICAN TRUST PUBLICATIONS
13- AVC	AUDIO-VISUAL CENTER
14- IBS	ISLAMIC BOOK SERVICE

15- MBA	MUSLIM BUSINESSMEN ASSOCIATION
16- MYNA	MUSLIM YOUTH OF NORTH AMERICA
17- IFC	ISNA FIQH COMMITTEE
18- IPAC	ISNA POLITICAL AWARENESS COMMITTEE
19- IED	ISLAMIC EDUCATION DEPARTMENT
20- MAYA	MUSLIM ARAB YOUTH ASSOCIATION
21- MISG	MALASIAN [sic] ISLAMIC STUDY GROUP
22- IAP	ISLAMIC ASSOCIATION FOR PALESTINE
23- UASR	UNITED ASSOCIATION FOR STUDIES AND RESEARCH
24- OLF	OCCUPIED LAND FUND
25- MIA	MERCY INTERNATIONAL ASSOCIATION
26- ISNA	ISLAMIC CIRCLE OF NORTH AMERICA
27- BMI	BAITUL MAL INC
28- IIIT	INTERNATIONAL INSTITUTE FOR ISLAMIC THOUGHT
29- IIC	ISLAMIC INFORMATION CENTER

SHARIAH
THE THREAT TO AMERICA
AN EXERCISE IN COMPETITIVE ANALYSIS
REPORT OF TEAM B II

For nearly a decade since 9/11, America's national security establishment's understanding of the threat of Islamic terrorism and its approach to contending with that danger flow directly from a conviction that they have nothing to do with Islam, except to the extent al Qaeda "perverts" or "hijacks" that religion.

But what if this characterization of the problem we continue to face nine years after 9/11 is simply and utterly wrong? What if there actually is a direct tie between what recognized, mainstream authorities of Islam call "shariah" and the jihad (or holy war) it demands of adherents, some of which is manifested as terrifying violence?

What if, in addition, jihadists engage in non-violent – and, in some ways, far more insidious – efforts to accomplish the same goal: the supremacy of shariah worldwide under a caliph?

These questions have been the focus of an intensive six-month study by a remarkable group of highly accomplished civilian and military national security professionals. Notable among its members are former Director of Central Intelligence R. James Woolsey, former Director of the Defense Intelligence Agency Lieutenant General Harry "Ed" Soyster, former Deputy Under Secretary of Defense for Intelligence Lieutenant General William G. "Jerry" Boykin and former Assistant U.S. Attorney Andrew C. McCarthy.

Together, this group has formed a "Team B," modeled after a similar initiative that supplied at a critical moment during the Cold War a second opinion on Soviet intentions and capabilities, a study that helped shape and underpin Ronald Reagan's efforts to challenge the form of appeasement of our totalitarian ideological foes known at the time as "détente." Ultimately, that Team B report helped underpin his strategy as President to take down the USSR.

Like its predecessor, today's Team B II has provided a dramatically divergent "second opinion" from the official U.S. government ("Team A") party line on the most important challenge of our time. Shariah: The Threat to America, counters the notion that the present totalitarian ideology bent on our destruction can be safely ignored, misconstrued or appeased in the name of the contemporary counterpart to détente: "engagement."

Shariah: The Threat to America demonstrates a troubling reality: The Obama administration and its immediate predecessors under both political parties – along with many state and local governments – have been blind, in some cases willfully so and in every case perilously so, to fundamental facts: the true nature of the enemy we confront; what actually animates him; the progress he is making towards achieving our destruction; and what we need to do to prevent his success.

This situation is dangerous in the extreme to our Constitution, freedoms, form of government and security. It must not be allowed to persist.

As a critical step toward the needed corrective, Team B II is proud to present its contribution to a long-overdue and urgently needed national debate about the true wellspring of jihadism: shariah. The findings of this study are as compelling as they are authoritative.

Shariah: The Threat to America **s available on paperback or Kindle at Amazon.com. For more information about this project, see securefreedom.org.**

THE MUSLIM BROTHERHOOD
IN AMERICA

A Course in 10 Parts
presented by FRANK GAFFNEY

Have you ever asked yourself why, despite more than ten years
of efforts –involving, among other things, the loss of thousands of lives
in wars in Iraq and Afghanistan, well-over a trillion dollars spent,
countless man-years wasted waiting in airport security lines and endless
efforts to ensure that no offense is given to seemingly permanently
aggrieved Muslim activists – are we no closer to victory in the so-called
"war on terror" than we were on 9/11?

Thankfully, we have been able to kill some dangerous bad
guys. The sad truth of the matter is that, by almost any other measure,
the prospect of victory is becoming more remote by the day. And no
one seems able to explain the reason.

In an effort to provide the missing answer, on April 24, the
Center for Security Policy is making available via the Internet a new,
free ten-part video course called "The Muslim Brotherhood in America: The Enemy Within." This course connects the proverbial dots,
drawing on a wealth of publicly available data and first-hand accounts
to present a picture that has, for over a decade, been obscured, denied
and suppressed:

America faces in addition to the threat of violent jihad another, even more toxic danger – a stealthy and pre-violent form of warfare
aimed at destroying our constitutional form of democratic government
and free society. The Muslim Brotherhood is the prime-mover behind
this seditious campaign, which it calls "civilization jihad."

**The Muslim Brotherhood in America is available on DVD at
Amazon and at securefreedom.org**

Made in the USA
Middletown, DE
17 April 2015